GO FOR IT!™

VOLLEYBALL

FOR BOYS AND GIRLS

START RIGHT AND PLAY WELL

by Bill Gutman

with Illustrations
by Ben Brown

MARSHALL CAVENDISH
CORPORATION

GREY CASTLE PRESS

Marshall Cavendish Edition, Freeport, New York.

Published by arrangement with Grey Castle Press, Lakeville, Ct.

Printed in the USA

The Library of Congress Cataloging in Publication Data

Gutman, Bill.
    Volleyball : start right and play well / by Bill Gutman ; with
illustrations by Ben Brown.
       p.   cm. — (Go for it!)
    Summary: Describes the history, current teams, leagues, and
championships of volleyball and provides instruction on how to play
the game.
    ISBN 0-942545-95-8 (lib. bdg.)
    1. Volleyball—Juvenile literature. [1. Volleyball.] I. Brown,
Ben, 1921–   Ill. II. Title. III. Series: Gutman, Bill. Go for
it!
GV1015.3.G87   1990
796.325—dc20   89-7584
                                                               CIP
                                                               AC

Photo credits: All-Sport U.S.A./Damian Strohmeyer, page 7, left and right.

Special thanks to: Carlo Billeci, varsity volleyball coach, Dover Junior/Senior High
School, Dover Plains, N.Y.

Picture research: Omni Photo Communications, Inc.

ABOUT THE AUTHOR

Bill Gutman is the author of over 70 books for children and young adults. The majority of his titles have dealt with sports, in both fiction and non-fiction, including "how-to" books. His name is well-known to librarians who make it their business to be informed about books of special interest to boys and reluctant readers. He lives in Poughquag, New York.

ABOUT THE ILLUSTRATOR

Ben Brown's experience ranges from cartoonist to gallery painter. He is a graduate of the High School of Music & Art in New York City and the University of Iowa Art School. He has been a member of the National Academy of Design and the Art Students' League. He has illustrated government training manuals for the disadvantaged (using sports as themes), and his animation work for the American Bible Society won two blue ribbons from the American Film Festival. He lives in Great Barrington, Massachusetts.

In order to keep the instructions in this book as simple as possible, the author has chosen in most cases to use "he" to signify both boys and girls.

A BRIEF HISTORY

The sport of volleyball may have come about because of the invention of another sport—basketball. In 1891, James Naismith invented basketball at the YMCA International Training School in Springfield, Massachusetts. Just four years later, in nearby Holyoke, Massachusetts, another game got its start.

William G. Morgan was the man who invented volleyball. He was the director of the Holyoke YMCA. In the winter of 1895, he began looking for a game that could be played in the physical education classes. The classes were getting larger and Morgan felt that the young people wanted something else to do.

Basketball, the young sport, seemed like the perfect choice. But William Morgan felt that the game was too rough. He thought about tennis. But not enough people could play at one time. Still, the idea of hitting a ball over a net seemed to be a good one. What if the players didn't need a bat or racket? What if they could just use their hands?

Morgan began playing with that idea. He started with a basketball, but it was too heavy to hit with the hands. Basketballs in those days had a lining called a bladder, which was put inside a leather covering. Morgan tried using just the bladder. That was better, but now the ball was a bit too light. Finally, he had one made by a local sporting goods company and then began developing his new sport.

Morgan liked the idea of a group of players hitting a ball back and forth across a net until the ball either touched the floor or went out of bounds. The first net was six feet, six inches off the ground. This was high enough to be above an average man's head. Of course, it has since been raised in the modern game.

At first, the game was also played in innings, and its name was "mintonette." This was because its inventor felt it looked a lot like badminton. But about a year later, a Springfield College professor watching the game suggested that it be called "volley ball." The name stuck.

By 1897, the sport had grown enough for the first set of rules to be published. From that point, the game was spread by the YMCA organization throughout the United States and in many other parts of the world. An American missionary, the Reverend F. H. Brown, helped to bring the sport to Japan in 1913. It started at a YMCA there, too, and soon became popular in that country.

But there were still growing pains. Like most new sports, the rules were different from place to place. By 1916, volleyball was no longer played by innings. Instead, 15 points won a game. Despite all the changes, there were already nearly a quarter of a million people playing the new game. There was a national championship tournament held for the first time in 1922, and in 1928, the United States Volleyball Association began.

The sport continued to grow through the 1940s and 1950s. But in the United States it was purely a recreational activity, a fun game. It was played in schools, at picnics, or at the beach. At that time, the game did not rank with any of the really competitive sports.

But in other countries the sport was being played hard by fine athletes, both men and women. Finally, in 1964, volleyball

Left. Volleyball today is a power game with jumping, rolling, and diving. But it still takes a soft touch to excel. Here, Jeff Stork of the United States National Team gets ready to set the ball to his leaping spiker. *Right.* Caren Kemner shows great form and jumping ability as she goes high in the air to spike the ball.

became part of the Olympic Games. With that, a new kind of volleyball was born.

It was the Japanese women's team that first showed everyone how volleyball could be played. The team was athletic and played the game in a new, exciting way. They leaped and ran, jumped and dove, and were all over the court. And they spiked or hit the ball as hard as they could. They not only won the gold medal, but also started a style of play known as "power volleyball."

Volleyball today can be played on several levels. It can be played almost anywhere, from backyard lawns to public parks and school phys-ed classes.

Then there is competitive volleyball, the kind played today at colleges, and in many local leagues, as well as in the Olympics. That's the power game, played by both men and women. It requires good athletes, a great deal of practice and teamwork, and a very high level of skill.

There is also co-ed volleyball, in which men and women play on the same team. This game is often played on the west coast, where there are beach leagues in many places. Beach volleyball has become an extremely popular version of the game. Diving and rolling on the soft sand is a lot easier than diving and rolling on a hard gymnasium floor.

So the sport that William Morgan devised nearly one hundred years ago has grown and flourished on a worldwide level. Volleyball is a game that can be played by everyone. And, unlike some other sports, volleyball can be fun from almost the very first day.

ORGANIZED VOLLEYBALL

The United States Volleyball Association (USVBA) has been the governing body for the sport since 1928. It has helped to develop great players who are as good as any in the world. In fact, the United States has won a number of Olympic Gold Medals in volleyball, proving that power volleyball is here to stay.

The sport is offered in schools all over the country, beginning at the elementary level. Young people can play the game strictly for fun, or can begin to learn the power game as they get older.

Those who become top players now have many opportunities to continue at the college level. There are many athletic scholarships available to volleyball players. Most schools have both men's and women's programs. In fact, since the laws regarding women's athletics were changed in 1972, college volleyball has become a popular and exciting sport for women.

The law change forced many schools to offer the same athletic scholarships to women as to men. That got things started, but since then the game has grown on its own. College programs have become better and better. There are more good players and topflight competition all over the land.

There has also been some professional volleyball activity. The

International Volleyball Assocation was formed in 1975. The teams came mostly from the Southwest and Pacific Coast. What made the league unique was that the teams were made up of both men and women.

Volleyball certainly has not become a major professional sport like baseball, football or basketball. But it has its own fans, many good players, and the potential for excitement. If the game continues to grow in popularity with the young people, professional volleyball can become even more widespread in the future.

The Game Of Volleyball

The standard volleyball court is 60 feet long by 30 feet wide. All lines are two inches wide, except for the center line, which measures four inches. The top of the net is 7¼ inches high for women and 8 feet for men. That's higher than when the game was first invented. The net for younger children is sometimes placed at 7 feet.

There is a spiking line on each side of the court, 10 feet from the center line. The standards, or posts, supporting the net are placed outside the lines of the court. There are two antennas that extend 2 feet, 8 inches higher than the net, right above the out-of-bounds line. The ball must pass over the net and between the antennas to remain in play.

The basic rules of the game are quite simple. A team must score 15 points to win a game. However, a team must win a game by at least two points. So a game that is at 15-14 must continue until one team has a two-point lead. Depending on the age level or league, either the best two-of-three or the best three-of-five games wins the match.

Only the team serving the ball can score a point. If they score,

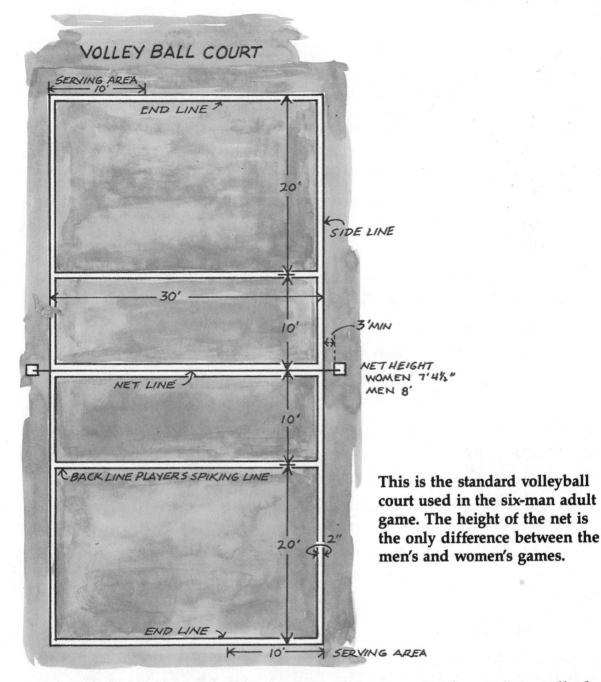

VOLLEY BALL COURT

SERVING AREA
10'

END LINE

20'

SIDE LINE

30'

10'

3' MIN

NET LINE

NET HEIGHT
WOMEN 7'4½"
MEN 8'

10'

BACK LINE PLAYERS SPIKING LINE

This is the standard volleyball court used in the six-man adult game. The height of the net is the only difference between the men's and women's games.

20'   2"

END LINE

10'   SERVING AREA

they continue serving. If they fail to score, a "side out" is called and the serve goes over to the other team. The game is played with six players on a side. Three are stationed in the front part of the court. They stand within the 10 foot spiking area. The other three are in the 20 foot area in the back part of the court.

The names for the positions are quite simple. The three

11

players in the back are the *left back, center back,* and *right back.* The front players are the *right front, center front* and *left front.* They are sometimes called the *left, right* and *center forwards.*

The player on the right side of the back row is the server. He must serve from behind the end line, within a serving area that extends 10 feet from the corner of the court (see drawing). But the same player does not serve each time his team gets the ball.

Unlike other sports, volleyball is a game in which players play all six positions. Because each time the team gets the ball back to serve, the players rotate one position. They move clockwise during the entire course of a match. Whichever player moves into the right back position is the one who serves. So during the course of the game, each player gets to play all six positions.

All the server must do is put the ball in play on the opponent's side of the net. He must hit it either underhand or overhand from the serving area. The ball has to clear the net and come down in bounds on the other side. It cannot touch the net or a player on the server's side. There is a coin toss before the game to determine which team serves first.

If the serve doesn't clear the net or goes out of bounds, it is no good and the other team gets the serve on a side out. But a point is not scored. But if the serve clears the net and stays in bounds, then the other team must play it.

The ball must always be hit before it lands on the court. Each team can hit the ball three times. The third hit, however, must put the ball over the net. The ball can also be put over the net on the first or second hit, but most teams take advantage of the three-hit rule. No one player can hit the ball two times in a row. Though if a second player makes the second hit, the first player can come back for the third hit.

Players are allowed to hit the ball with hands, fists, arms, or any part of the body from the waist up. However, catching,

12

cradling, scooping and throwing the ball is illegal. If a point is scored on the serve, the team continues to serve. In fact, the same player serves until his team fails to win a point. The players rotate only when the other team loses its serve. Then there is a new server.

Points are scored when the ball hits the floor on the opponent's side of the net or when an opponent returns it into the net or out of bounds. A point can also be scored on a foul. For example, a foul will be called if a player reaches over the net to play a ball (this does not include a follow through on a spike or block). A player crossing the center line while the ball is in play has also committed a foul. If a player touches the net during a point, a foul will be called. And a player out of position on the court during play can be called for a foul.

These are some of the more common fouls. A single referee calls the game and the fouls. He stands on a platform at one side of the net. However, the ref can be assisted by an umpire, who will be at court level on the side opposite the referee. There can also be two or four linesmen at the corners. Their jobs are mainly to make in or out calls as the ball hits the court.

The strategy of the game is very basic. Each team always tries to take the maximum three hits. And each hit has a purpose. So there is a pattern to the sequence every time.

The first player to get the ball makes a pass. The purpose of the pass is to get the ball to a teammate who will set up the all-important third hit. So the second hit is called the *set*. The purpose of the set is to loft the ball near the net so a front court player can make the third hit. The third hit is usually an exciting, leaping shot called a *spike*.

It is the spike that gives a team its best chance to win a point. The spiker leaps high in the air, timing his jump so he can take a hard swing as the ball comes down just above the net. He is trying to hit the ball so hard that no one from the other team will be able to return it.

Because a well-hit spike is so hard to return, the defense team has a maneuver of its own to try to stop the spike before it gets over the net. They send one, two or sometimes three players high in the air to block it just as it comes off the spiker's hand. If they do it right, the ball will bounce right back into the offensive court.

If the defensive team cannot block the spike, one of the players must try to get the ball before it hits the floor. This sometimes takes an exciting defensive maneuver like a dive or roll. If one of the defenders can get the ball in the air, then a teammate will try to set the ball for a spiking try from one of his teammates.

So the pattern is repeated often during a game. Pass, set and spike. An attempt to block. Pass, set, spike, over and over again. That's why it takes quick, skilled players to compete at the top level of the sport.

Because volleyball has become so popular everywhere, there are some new and different forms of the game. Young people under 16 are classified as junior players. They play with a 7-foot net and a lighter ball. Other changes include allowing juniors two serves instead of one. They also may serve from the center of the end line instead of the right corner.

Junior play also allows for varying numbers of players on each team. The six-person game is played on a smaller court, 40 feet long by 20 feet wide. There is a nine-person game, usually played on a 50×25 foot court; and even a 12-person game played on a 60×30 foot area. These types of games allow more young people to participate, especially in large gym classes.

On the California beaches, local players often participate in doubles volleyball. It is played on a 50×25 foot court with just two players on a team. Needless to say, the players must be cat-quick and willing to dive and roll all over the court to get the ball. Who knows, with the sport still growing all over the world, there may soon be another new version of the game.

Uniform And Equipment

Volleyball equipment is not fancy or expensive. The ball itself is soft and light. It is usually white in color. The newer balls have a leather covering, and unlike the older balls, the seams are not sewn. They are joined together by a process called "vulcanization." That allows the ball to keep its shape and last longer than the older ones.

A regulation volleyball should be from 25 5/8 to 26 3/8 inches in circumference (the distance around the ball) and should weigh between 9 and 10 ounces. As mentioned earlier, juniors sometimes play with a ball that weighs just 6 to 7 ounces.

Uniforms, too, are very basic. Both boys and girls wear shorts, a jersey, socks and shoes. Clothing, of course, should fit well and be a bit on the loose side so it doesn't restrict the players' movement. And there are a couple of extra pieces that players in today's power game usually wear.

The standard volleyball weighs between 9 and 10 ounces and measures between 25 5/8 and 26 3/8 inches in circumference. Juniors sometimes play with a smaller and lighter ball.

The volleyball uniform is quite simple. Shorts, shirt and shoes are the basics. But in the power volleyball game of today, many players choose to wear kneepads. Many also wear long-sleeved shirts to help avoid scrapes and bruises from diving and rolling on the court.

Many volleyball players today prefer to wear a longsleeved jersey because of the many forearm passes they must make. Rather than have the ball constantly banging off their forearms, they wear long-sleeved jerseys, which also protect the elbows and forearms on dives and rolls.

Not all players will wear long sleeves, however. Some still prefer the natural feel of the ball hitting their arms. But almost every volleyball player today (except those playing on beaches) wears kneepads. With all the diving and rolling, the knees will definitely contact the court hard during the course of a game.

The final item is the shoes. As with all other sports today, there are shoes or sneakers made specially for volleyball. Many of these volleyball sneakers have an added support around the heel and ankle part of the shoe called the collar. This protects the ankle and the Achilles' tendon.

Because of the constant jumping, shoes should also be well cushioned in the sole and have a good arch support. And, of course, they must fit well. There are many different brands of shoes, as well as different styles. As a rule, nylon and polyester shoes last the longest and are generally not as expensive as leather shoes.

There should also be some extra support on each side of the toes. This will help the shoe hold up to the quick, side-to-side movement that volleyball calls for. A good sole is the rippled or ridged sole, which will produce the best traction on indoor volleyball courts.

Don't let shoe selection drive you crazy. Buy the best shoe you can afford and make sure it fits well. Now you're almost ready to play.

Getting Ready To Play

Power volleyball is a fast and action-filled game. There are quick stops and starts, as well as a great deal of jumping, diving and rolling. Players have to be in condition to play the sport, and must know how to get ready before each practice and game.

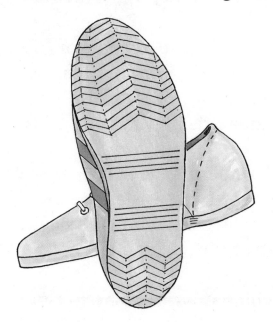

Most volleyball shoes have rippled or ridged soles to give the player good traction on indoor courts. The better shoes also have special supports for the heel and ankle, and should be well-cushioned in the heel. That's because of all the jumping volleyball players must do during a game.

If you plan on playing volleyball for the first time, you must make sure you are in shape before you even start. Otherwise, you may pull a muscle or suffer some other kind of injury. At the very least, you will be quite tired and sore. So it's best to get ready even before that first practice.

That means getting your body ready to play. If you are active and already play sports, you should be in pretty good shape. Then, your volleyball coach can tell you the best exercises to get ready for his sport.

But if you haven't been very active, you should start with a regular running program. By jogging several miles three or four times a week, you will begin to build up your stamina. Another good exercise before you start your new sport is jumping rope. Volleyball involves a great deal of jumping, and working with the rope will get your leg muscles ready. It will also help your coordination and quickness.

Pushups, pullup, and situps will also help. These are very basic exercises and will help you get stronger and in overall good condition. The rest of your daily routine should also be geared to athletics. That means eating the right foods and getting enough rest.

Learn to divide your time so you can do your schoolwork, help around the house and still have time to work out, eat right and get a good night's sleep. Things such as tobacco, alcohol and drugs can only hurt you, both in sports and in your everyday life. Be smart and say no.

As with other sports, volleyball players must be sure to warm up before each practice session and game. The easiest way to pull a muscle is to play a sport like volleyball without stretching and warming up. Some light jogging and stretching exercises are a good way to start.

There are a number of good stretching exercises players can

By lying on your back, then sitting up slowly and reaching forward until you can grab your feet, you work stomach and leg muscles. All stretching exercises should be done slowly and held for five to 10 seconds at the maximum point of the stretch.

do. Each coach may have his favorites that he will want his players to follow.

The important thing is to stretch all the main muscle groups. What is important is to find a routine and stick with it. Always stretch before you practice or play. Never start playing cold. Remember, all stretching exercises should be done slowly. Hold the final position for five to ten seconds. If there is pain or discomfort, stop.

All volleyball players should stretch and warm-up before practice and games. There are many good exercises that every player can do. A coach usually has his own routine. One good exercise is to lie flat on the ground, then raise your legs slowly over your head until they touch the ground behind you. This exercise will stretch leg, stomach and back muscles.

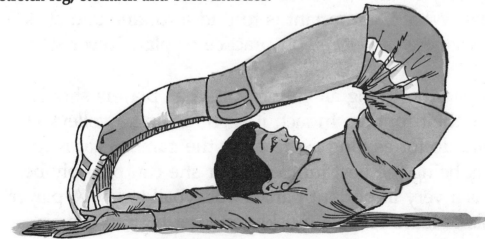

Good jumping ability is very important to every volleyball player. It is a
skill that can be improved upon with
practice. One good way to do this is to
find a way to see how high you jump.
Then keep trying to go higher. The
more jumping the better, because you
must jump just as high late in the
game as you do early in the game.

The important thing is to stretch all the main muscle groups.
It's not necessary to do the exercises described here. They are
just examples. What is important is to find a routine and stick
with it. Always stretch before you practice or play. Never start
playing cold.

There is one other thing all young volleyball players should
do as part of their routine. In fact, it is something a volleyball
player should do for as long as he plays the game. That is to
work hard at being the best jumper he or she can possibly be.

Jumping is a very important part of volleyball today. A player
must be able to leave his feet quickly and get high in the air.

Since spiking and blocking are such a big part of the power game, a player who cannot jump well won't be able to compete.

There are some people who can naturally jump higher than others. But anyone can improve his jumping by working at it. In fact, some feel that a player working hard on his jumping can improve by perhaps three or four inches in a single season.

To begin with, any exercise that strengthens the leg muscles will help your jumping. Simple rope jumping will increase your stamina and endurance, while also toning and strengthening the jumping muscles in the legs. Doing squats and jump squats is still another way to do this. A jump squat is just what it sounds like. Instead of coming back to a standing position after squatting down, spring out of the squat and jump as high as you can once you straighten up. When you come down, go right back into a squat and do it again.

The final piece of advice is to simply jump. Pick a target, a pole, a wall, the backboard on a basketball court. Then take two quick steps and leap as high as you can, touching a spot on your target. Then mark the point of your highest leap. Each time you jump after that, try to touch the target point or go above it.

Because you will jump many times during a volleyball game, you should repeat this jumping drill often. You've got to be able to jump as high during the last part of the game as at the beginning. If you tire, you won't go as high. And in a close game, that might hurt your team. So the better shape you're in when you begin playing the game, the better player you will become.

LEARNING TO PLAY VOLLEYBALL

Learning How To Serve

A good serve is very important to becoming a successful volleyball player. While a beginner might just want to put the ball in play, a top player is like a baseball pitcher. He will deliver the ball across the net in several different ways. By doing that, he can keep the defensive team off balance and give his team a much better chance to score points.

The top servers can make the ball spin and curve, dart and drift. If the opposition doesn't know what is coming next, it's harder to get ready for a return. All these serves are made with an overhand motion. But for young players just starting, the basic underhand serve is the best to use.

For the beginner, putting the ball in play is the most important thing. The other kinds of serves will come later. Remember, if you don't get the ball in play, your team cannot score a point and they also lose the serve. So even a beginner should be able to put at least seven out of 10 serves in play.

It's easy to practice serving. All that is needed is two players standing on opposite sides of the court. They can practice serving to each other as long as they wish. If they have five volleyballs with them, each can serve five times. Then the other person can hit them back.

Players using the underhand serve often hit the ball with a closed fist. The ball should contact the flat part of the fingers between the knuckles and the heel of the hand at the same time.

As mentioned already, most young players begin with the underhand serve. The reason is simple. It is the easiest to learn and control. There are two ways to hit the underhand serve. A player may strike the ball with his fist or with the heel of the open hand. Most coaches prefer the heel of the open hand.

The server, of course, must stand behind the 10-foot wide serving area at the right corner of the court. Some servers like to stand just behind the end line, while others stand several feet behind. Remember, you cannot step on that line until you have hit the ball. If you do, a *foot fault* will be called and you will lose the ball for your team. Whenever the serving team loses the ball, it is called a *side out*.

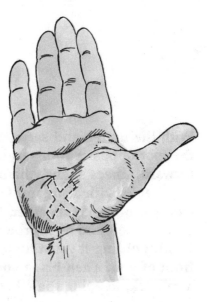

A player using his open hand with the underhand serve should contact the ball with the heel of the hand only. The important thing is to strike the ball with a flat surface, and that takes practice.

23

If you use the underhand serve, your motion should be the same each time. Begin by standing in the serving area with a comfortable stance. Your knees should be bent slightly. Some players prefer to start with a square stance. Others feel better if the foot opposite their serving hand is closer to the front court.

The ball should be held or balanced on the palm of the non-hitting hand, waist high and out in front of your body. Start the motion by swinging your hitting arm back, elbow straight. At this point, there are two ways to complete the serve.

If you start with your opposite foot in front, you will not take a step. Instead, you will shift your weight from the back foot to

With the underhand serve, begin with the foot opposite your serving hand forward, knees slightly bent. You can also begin with a square stance (not shown), both feet together. Balance the ball on the palm of your non-hitting hand, holding it waist high and out in front of you. Then bring your hitting arm back, keeping the elbow straight.

the front as you bring your arm forward. If you start with the square stance, you will take a short step with your opposite foot as you begin the swing and the weight shift.

As your hitting hand begins to swing past your body, release the ball and make contact out in front of your body. Contact can be made with the top of the knuckles and heel of the fist, or just the heel of the open hand. As the weight shift is completed to the front foot and contact is made, complete the follow through with your arm.

A short follow through will allow the ball to float over the net with little or no spin. That will cause the ball to dip and dance,

Unless you started with a square stance, you won't have to stride. (With the square stance, you will take a short step with the leg opposite the hitting hand. Simply shift your weight from the rear to the front as you begin the swing. When the hitting hand passes your body, release the ball from the opposite hand and make contact out in front of your body. As contact is made with the knuckles and heel of the fist, complete the weight shift and follow through with your arm.

something like a knuckleball in baseball. This serve is called an *underhand floater.* A longer follow through will put spin on the ball and it will go over the net on a straight arc. Since accuracy is most important at the beginning, use the style that puts the ball in play most often.

Some coaches feel that if you are going to serve underhand, the short follow through and floater is a better serve. The slight changes in the flight of the ball will be just enough to give you a bit of an edge. But whichever style you use, always be sure to keep your eye on the ball until right after you have made contact. If you bring your head up too soon, there is more of a chance of a mis-hit ball.

Almost every player who continues with volleyball will sooner or later begin to serve overhand. The overhand serve can be hit with more power. Also, the ball can be made to do more "tricks" as it goes over the net. Accuracy is still important. A missed serve is a wasted opportunity. But with the overhand style, the server is hoping for a better chance to win the point.

Perhaps the most popular serve in volleyball is the *overhand floater.* Like the underhand floater, the overhand floater will dip and dance, again in knuckleball fashion. It never moves the same way twice.

Players generally start three or four feet behind the serving line. Because they will step into the ball, they want to avoid a foot fault. Some players will stand even further back. They feel the longer distance will allow the ball to move more as it clears the net. Distance is something all players must decide upon as they become more experienced.

You should begin by facing the net with feet comfortably apart. The foot opposite the hitting hand should be a short distance in front of the other. The ball should be held about waist high out in front of your body. The tossing hand is

With the overhand serve, begin in a comfortable position perhaps three or four feet behind the serving line. The foot opposite the hitting hand is usually a little in front of the other. The ball should be balanced on the tossing hand, with the hitting hand poised at about shoulder height.

underneath, the hitting hand on top. As with the serve in tennis, the toss is very important for a good serve.

The toss should be between two and three feet in the air, or slightly above the highest point you can reach. the ball should be about a step in front of the hitting shoulder. Next, you should stride forward and begin to shift your weight from the rear to the front foot. At the same time, bring your hitting hand back to a position just behind the ear. This is done by bending the arm at the elbow.

As the ball starts down, bring your hitting arm up over the top, leading with the elbow then straightening it suddenly. Contact with the ball is made slightly in front of the body. The heel

Left. The weight should be on the back foot at the beginning of the toss. As your arm comes up with the ball, begin bringing your hitting hand up and back.

Right. The toss should be slightly above the top of your reach, with the ball just out in front of the hitting shoulder. The player here has already taken a stride with her left foot and has her arm behind her left ear, bent at the elbow.

Right. The hit is made by leading with the elbow, then straightening it quickly. Contact should be made with the heel of the hand just out in front of the body. In serving a floater, which has little or no spin, there is very little follow through. The stroke is like a short punch. To put spin on the serve, a longer follow through is used.

Left. As you start your swing, you will also begin to shift your weight from back to front. The ball should be hit just as it begins its downward fall.

of the hand should hit just below the center of the ball. This will provide lift to get it up and over the net.

Once again, the follow through is limited. The floating serve is almost a punching action. That way, there will be no spin on the ball and it will have uneven movement. With all your weight now on the front foot, the back foot can be brought forward as you move onto the court to get into action.

The basic motion for the overhead floater is the same motion used for all overhead serves. The difference in the serve comes from the way in which the ball is struck.

One variation of the overhead flat, or floating, serve is the *overhead spin serve.* The same motion is used as with the overhead floater. That way, the defensive team will not know which type of serve is coming until the ball is hit. The difference is in the contact and follow through.

At contact, the heel of the hand will hit the ball slightly off center. Unlike the motion for the overhead flat serve, the server now snaps his wrist, allowing his fingers to make contact with the ball. It is the motion of the fingers across the ball that gives it spin. A good topspin serve will dip just after it crosses the net. Topspin comes from the hand rolling over the top of the ball as contact is made. Experienced servers can also vary their hand position to make the ball break to the right or left.

The follow through with the spin serve is more complete. In fact, instead of stopping right after contact, the serving arm is brought down and across the front of the body. This follow through is similar to a pitcher making an overhand delivery.

Once you have learned to put your serve in play most of the time, you can then work on placing it in certain spots on the court. As a rule, serves should always go deep. The closer to the backline, the better. Serves that go deep along the side lines are probably the most difficult to return well.

That's because the returner must first decide whether the serve will be in or out. A wrong decision can cost the team a point. And when the ball must be passed from deep in the corner, the serving team can almost predict where the spike will come from. Then they will be in a better position to block.

A good server in volleyball may not have as much control over the game as a good server in tennis. But it is still important to practice serving all the time. Accuracy is the most important thing. Put your serves in play. Then develop a variety. A single type of serve, no matter how good, will not give your team the edge, if you use it all the time. But if you can mix your serves, the defense will have to adjust.

Always use the same serving motion. That gives you better control and accuracy. It will also keep your opponents from knowing what kind of serve is coming. Do all these things and you will find yourself helping your team each time you step up to the serving line.

Learning How To Pass

The way a team receives a serve is a very important part of volleyball. It marks the change-over from defense to offense. In today's power volleyball, the first hit a team makes is called *the pass*. It is made by contacting the ball on the lower part of the forearms near the wrists.

This may sound strange at first, but it has become the standard way to make the pass, which is the first of the three hits that every team tries to make. The basic forearm pass is called the *bump pass*.

With the forearm pass, the object is to make a flat surface with the forearms. To do this, players must begin by locking

With the basic forearm, or bump pass, the player approaches the ball low, with knees bent and one foot out in front of the other. The hands have come forward, ready to get into the passing position. And the eyes are firmly fixed on the flight of the ball.

The passer has now locked his hands, using the palm grip, and has straightened his elbows. His forearms are then brought close together to make the hit. The player is also "looking" the ball right onto his arms.

their hands. There are a number of ways to do this, but here are three popular ways that a young player can try.

First, make a fist with one hand. Then wrap the fingers of the other hand around the fist with the thumbs together on top and pointing away from you. Another way is to simply interlock the four fingers of each hand with the thumbs on top. The third method involves cupping the fingers of one hand inside the palm of the other hand. Once again, the thumbs come together on top of the hands, as they did with the two other methods.

The actual pass is made with the hands locked and forearms

The hit is made just above the wrists on the forearms. The forearms should be even with one another to avoid the change of a double hit. A slight lift of the knees and gentle lift of the arms is all that is needed for the basic hit. The force of the ball coming down from a hard serve will cause it to rebound sharply off the arms. The follow through should just be a steady flow, with both legs and arms continuing their rise.

out in front. The elbows are also straight and locked. They should also be pressed inward, so that the forearms are as close to one another as possible. If the forearms do not form a flat surface, you can be called for a *double hit,* which is a foul. Or if the hands separate at contact, a double hit may also be called.

Some players prefer to contact the ball near the wrist. Others would rather have the contact higher on the forearms. They feel that the lower forearms are too small to make a large enough flat surface for a good hit. Again, this is something all players must practice. Younger players might well find that it's better to make the contact higher on the forearms. But your coach can always advise you about this.

The important part of the bump pass is to just meet the ball gently. There's no reason to swing hard at it. A hard serve will have enough momentum to rebound off the locked forearms and still go where you want it to go. So, again, it is a matter of learning the right technique.

A player making a pass must be ready to use quick footwork. The object is to be in the spot where the ball is coming down. That way, you won't have to reach or lunge for a ball that moves away at the last second. So don't make that final move until you are sure where the ball will be. Then, a quick step or two will put you right where you want to be.

The pass should be made from the *ready-to-pass position.* This means having your hands locked and elbows close together. Your feet should be spread wide enough to give you good balance. One foot should always be a little in front of the other. Knees should be bent, or flexed, to about a 90-degree angle.

As the ball comes down, drop your arms, but not too close to the floor. The swing is not a hard one. Bring your body up from the knees and at the same time make an almost gentle lift with your arms. The lift should be made from the shoulders. The follow through should be a slow and steady rise of both arms and legs. For a slower moving ball that has to be hit high, you will want to swing your arms more and follow through to a higher position.

The pass should be a soft one that can be easily controlled by the *setter*, the player who will be hitting the ball next. By receiving different kinds of serves, you'll soon get a feel for making a good pass to your setter. Talking with teammates always helps. If you are getting into a bad habit, or making a low pass that is hard to handle, another teammate should tell you.

Remember, a volleyball player takes a turn at each position. While you might be the passer on one turn, you'll soon be the setter on another. So try to give the setter the kind of pass you would want when you are the setter.

The *elbow snap* is a slightly different type of forearm pass. It is normally used by experienced players. As a rule, young and inexperienced players should not use it. There is more chance for a mis-hit than with the bump pass. But it doesn't hurt to know how the elbow snap is done.

As the ball approaches, the ready position is the same as with the bump pass. The hands are locked together, but the elbows remain bent. As the arms are dropped to get ready to meet the ball, the passer begins the elbow snap. He does this by locking his elbows and bringing them together in a snapping motion a split second before contacting the ball. Contact is the same as with the bump pass, and so is the follow through.

Players who use the elbow snap feel that it allows them to remain more relaxed on the court, not as tight and tense. But for young players, it should only be tried after they have become quite good at the basic bump pass.

Of course, not every ball is going to come right at the passer. There are some other types of passes that every player will have to make sooner or later.

One of the skills that should be practiced is passing the ball to the side. This has to be done when the setter is not directly in front of you. The technique is the same, except for some basic changes. For example, here's how to pass the ball to a setter on the right. Do not turn your body in the direction of the pass. As you get down to make contact, lower your right shoulder and bend the knee closest to the net. Tilt your forearms to the right, still keeping the hands and elbows locked. Then make the hit as you normally would.

Of course, there are going to be times when the ball comes across the net too fast for a player to get set for a normal bump pass. In these cases, the player must try to make a *one-hand pass*. This is not an ideal play, but it's better than letting the ball hit the floor for a point.

The one-hand pass can be made with a fist or open hand. The key is to get down low and keep the arm straight. The best thing is to try to contact the ball with the wrist or just above it with the forearm. Don't try anything fancy. Just get the ball high

There are times when a player just can't make the standard bump pass. Instead, she must keep the ball in the air any way she can. Hitting a ball just before it strikes the court is called digging. The one-hand dig is made by lunging sideways, getting low to the court, and punching the ball back in the air with the fist. The dig does not allow as much control as a bump pass, but at least it can keep the ball from hitting the floor and stopping play.

enough in the air so one of your teammates has a chance to play it.

Two keys to successful passing are to always watch the ball and to talk with your teammates. You can yell, "I got it!" or "My ball!" or anything else that tells the players near you that you've got it. Before the game, you might want to discuss who will take balls that are between you and a teammate. The more often that teammates work together, the better the team will be.

Remember, passing is a very important part of volleyball. A good pass puts the receiving team right back on the offense. A poor one leaves them in a defensive position, unable to get the offense started. If a single player on the team cannot make a good bump pass from all angles, that person will become a weak link. It won't take long for a team of good servers to always put the ball in that player's area.

So practice passing. Bump the ball off a wall if there is no one else around. Or practice with one or more of your teammates. The important thing is that you practice and become better.

Learning How To Set

Sometimes the setter is the forgotten person in a volleyball attack. It is the passer who starts the attack and the spiker who finishes it. In the middle is the setter. If he does his job right, he is sometimes hardly noticed. If he doesn't do it right, everyone knows he has stopped the attack sequence.

To many, the setter is like a quarterback. How setters do their job can be the difference between winning and losing the match. The setter must have a real feel for the game. He or she must also have speed and great reflexes, and know how to predict where the play will come. All this just to make a soft hit, but one that must be in perfect position for the spiker.

As the pass goes in the air, the setter moves into place to play

During volleyball action, players should always be in the ready position. This means knees bent and hands out in front. Players should also be on the balls of their feet so they can move quickly in any direction. And they should always make sure to watch the ball.

the ball. As it begins to come down, he gets into the *ready position*. That means being under the ball, feet spread comfortably apart, weight equal on both feet. The setter faces the direction in which the ball will go, then bends slightly at the knees.

Both hands should be up, about ten inches above the face. The fingers should be spread to make a "window" between the thumb and forefinger of each hand. That way, the setter can watch the ball come right into his hands.

In making a set, contact with the hands is all-important. The ball should hit the pads of the fingers very softly. If you give a little with yours hands, elbows and knees, you should get the right feel for the ball. It should never touch the palms of your hands during a set.

The ball is only on the fingertips for a fraction of a second. It is thrust back into the air by straightening the fingers, wrists and arms in a quick, snapping movement. The hands should be rotated inward as the ball comes down and outward as it is pushed away. The feet stay on the ground during the set.

Perhaps the biggest part of a good set is to relax the hands and wrists at contact. This allows the ball to settle into the hands for that instant before it is pushed back out. If this is done, the ball will not be batted away, but rather pushed out softly.

The object of the set, of course, is to prepare the spiker. Try to give the spiker a high trajectory. That will give him time to approach the net and jump high to get the ball. The ball may soar 6 to 12 feet above the net and come down very close to the top of the net—on your side, of course. For a team with smaller players, the ball should be set a few feet back from the net. That way, a smaller player can still spike the ball, using top spin, even though his hand is not above the net.

There are a number of basic sets. For the *front set*, the setter will get under and just behind the ball, then wait for it to come down. He will set it in the direction he is facing. Most sets are made in this manner. A good pass will allow a player to get in position for a front set.

Most front sets should be hit with a high trajectory. That will allow the spiker to make his approach and leap. In these cases, the setter is usually two or three feet from the net. So the ball will travel parallel to the net.

A second type of set is called the *back set*. The back set uses the same motions as the front set until contact is made with the ball. At contact, the setter must arch his back and direct the ball over his head to a spiker coming in behind him. The feet are kept on the ground and the ball is usually not set as high as with the front set.

The back set is often used to try to fool the blockers on the

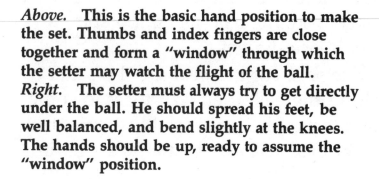

Above.   This is the basic hand position to make the set. Thumbs and index fingers are close together and form a "window" through which the setter may watch the flight of the ball.
Right.   The setter must always try to get directly under the ball. He should spread his feet, be well balanced, and bend slightly at the knees. The hands should be up, ready to assume the "window" position.

other team. If the setter is the center forward, he may face his left forward and appear to be getting ready for a front set. The blockers on the other team may commit too soon and move to block a spike from the left forward. If the setter spots them in time, he can then switch to the back set and push the ball over his head to the right forward. When this is done smoothly, the right forward may have a nearly unopposed spike.

Sometimes, the setter will receive the ball with his back to the

40

Just before contact, the setter relaxes both hands and wrists. The ball will then settle onto the fingertips for just a split second. It should never touch the palms. The setter should also give slightly with his hands, elbows and knees. The object is to have the ball hit the fingertips very softly.

The set is made by straightening fingers, wrists and arms. The movement is a quick, snapping one, thrusting the ball back into the air. The hands, which should be rotated inward as the ball approaches, are rotated outward as the ball is set. That way, the ball will not simply be batted away.

The back set is used when the spiker is behind the setter. To get the ball in position for a spike, the setter must deliver the ball back over his head. As the ball comes down, he should assume the front set position. The difference is that he will arch his back and contact the ball directly above his forehead. That way he will be able to set the ball behind him.

net. He will then have to set it to the right or left. To do this, he will use the *side set*. The trick is not to let the other team know which way the ball will go until the last possible instant. That sometimes means carrying it on the hands a split second longer than normal. So a setter runs the risk of a foul.

When the setter decides which way he wants to push the ball, he simply drops the correct shoulder and pushes the ball in that direction. Side setting is not easy and is not one of the sets a beginner should worry about learning. Once he has experience, then he can begin to work on the side set.

There are also times when the setter will have to jump for a ball. This doesn't happen often, but a good setter can sometimes fake a spike, then set for his teammate.

There will also be times when the setter may have to drop to his knees or even a sitting position to get under a ball. To set low like this means stronger wrist and arm action. This, too, is something that takes practice. You may not have to do it often. But you never know what will happen in a game and you always have to be ready.

Any player getting ready to set knows how important his job is. Setting keys the offense. That's why a setter must know how to handle all kinds of passes. He must practice until he knows what to do almost without thinking. For the setter is the busiest player on the court. One second, he is moving up for the pass. The next, he is hustling back on defense. That's why fast feet are very important.

So is knowing where the spikers are at all times. The setter must also know just where his spikers like to receive the ball. Like a quarterback, he must read the defense and take charge of the offense. It's an important job.

Learning How To Spike

It is the spike that most often brings volleyball fans to their feet. A good spiker leaps high in the air and slams the ball over the net with incredible force. Spiking is the way most points are scored during a match. The spike is the final link in the chain that includes the pass and set. It takes special skills to become a good spiker.

As a rule, spikers are the tallest players on the team. But the ability to jump high is even more important. A smaller player who can really leap can be a better spiker than the taller player who can't get off the ground. A player must also have a very good sense of timing. He must know when to jump so that he can spike the ball at just the right time.

There are four stages to the spike. They are the *approach*, the *jump*, the *attack* and the *recovery*. A young player must practice all four separately. Then he can begin to put them together. And one thing is for certain: the perfect spike is an electrifying play to watch.

Generally, the spike is hit as hard as possible. But there are also times when a spiker will hit the ball at half speed, or just dump the ball softly over the net. That type of soft shot is called a *dink* and is used to keep the defense off balance.

The approach usually consists of two to four long strides toward the net. Players with only average jumping ability will need the extra stride. The spiker's ready position can be up to 10 to 12 feet from the net. Some get as close as seven feet. The trick is to be able to judge the height and speed of the set. As a rule, the spiker doesn't move until the ball comes off the setter's hand. Then he suddenly explodes into his approach and jump.

Sometimes a last-second adjustment in the approach is needed. The spiker will take a short hop to get his steps just right. That's why it's important to know just where you are on the court and how many steps you'll need to get into spiking position. The approach can be from the left or right, or even from straight ahead. Each spiker has a favorite way of approaching the net.

The spiker's entire body must aid in the jump if he is to reach

Good spiking takes both timing and physical ability. Most spikers will take from two to four long steps as they approach the net. Some stand as close as 7 feet from the net, others as far as 10 or 12 feet. But they all watch the ball closely and are ready to explode to the net.

the maximum height. All spikers should jump with both feet, much like a diver going off a board. One reason for this is that the spiker must jump upward, not forward. Spikers taking off with two feet feel they have better control of the jump.

Your arms must also be a big part of the jump. Just before planting yourself for the take off, swing both arms behind your body, then drive them forward and upward into the jump. The arms should end up in the air, leading the rest of your body in the jump.

Now it's time to swing, or attack the ball. While in mid-air, aim the non-hitting arm at the ball and bring the hitting arm back behind your head. When you bend your elbow, you should look like a catcher getting ready to throw a baseball. Just

Right. Then, just before the hit is made, the legs and non-hitting arm are driven downward. This will let the striking arm reach its full extension. The spike begins with the elbow leading the arm into the ball.

Left. The jump takes a great deal of energy. Many spikers like to jump off both feet. This helps them jump upward instead of forward. At the takeoff, the arms are thrust upward. This, too, helps with the jump and also gets the arms in position for the spike. The non-hitting arm is pointed toward the ball, while the hitting arm is drawn back behind the head.

Left. The spiker gets his power from a quick snap of the upper arm at the elbow. Contact is with the heel of the open hand.

Right. As the arm drives into the ball, the wrist is snapped forward for power and direction. This also puts top spin on the ball, and that can make it even easier for the spiker to put the ball just where he wants it.

47

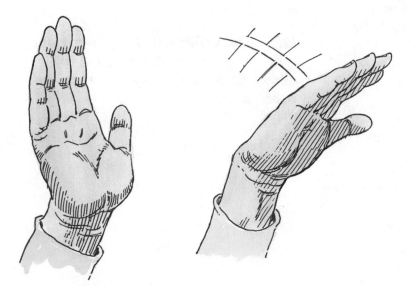

This is the basic movement of the hands during a hard spike. The snap of the wrist not only gives the spike added power, but also directs the ball down onto the court.

before starting the spiking action, you should drive both your legs and non-hitting arm downward. This allows the striking arm to reach full extension.

The elbow should lead the arm toward the ball. The power then comes from a rapid snap of the upper arm at the elbow. Contact is made with the heel of the open hand. At contact, the spiker snaps his wrist hard, putting topspin on the ball. The spin makes it easier for the spiker to place the ball where he wants it.

It is also the spin that brings the ball downward. The closer the ball is to the net at contact, the more you should make contact on the top side of the ball. This type of ball is hit more in front of the body. But even on close balls, you cannot let your jump take you into or under the net.

You cannot relax after making the hit. You must come down squarely from your jump, using your feet and knees to make a soft landing. It is important to be ready to recover your spike if it is blocked. It might come right back over the net to you. When that happens, you have to be ready to make a pass or a set. That is the recovery part of the spike.

These are the basic techniques for spiking. There are many

other things young players will learn as they get experience. To become a good basic spiker takes lots of practice. Players should practice their approach and jump from several different angles. They should also practice spiking with either arm.

For a righthander, the most power comes when he hits from the left corner of the net. He should angle the shot to the opposite corner of the opponent's court. The spiker also has to learn to watch the blockers. Their position can affect where he hits. If they're blocking him from going to the opposite side, he may try to put the ball between them. Or he can try to put the ball down the left sideline. That's why accuracy is so important. The

The dink shot is like a change of pace in baseball. The player approaches the net and leaps into the air as if he's going to spike. But at the last second, he just places the ball softly over the net. The object is to catch the defense off guard and dump the ball into an open area of the court.

spiker must be able to make these minor adjustments while in the air and hit to the open spot.

Another option is the dink. This is like a change of pace in baseball. The dink is a soft placement shot that should look exactly like a spike until the instant the ball is hit. If a spiker cannot fool the defense, a dink will not work. It could even lead to the loss of a point or a side out and loss of serve.

The only difference between the spike and the dink is the hit itself. The spiker does not use the heel of his hand. Instead, he uses the tips of his fingers to control the ball. But it must be a hit. If you balance the ball on your fingertips, you'll be called for a *held ball,* a foul. Many players try to place the dink shot just over the heads of the blockers so it falls behind them. Sometimes, you may have to angle the ball to the left or right.

Do not use the dink too often. It's a shot used once in a while to keep the defense off balance. It's real purpose is to make the spike more effective.

Spiking is just part of a complete volleyball package. But for many people, it's the most exciting part of the game. To be able to spike well is a real thrill. If you practice long and hard enough, you should be able to make it happen.

Learning How To Block

How do you stop a hard-hit spike? The best way is the *block,* the most important defensive play in volleyball. Blocking is something that calls for individual skill. But it also calls for teamwork.

All three players on the front line are allowed to block. Great timing is needed to leap high in the air to stop or at least deflect the spike as it rockets over the net. A well-spiked volleyball can travel at upwards of 70 miles per hour. So the blocking move must be almost perfect to stop it. That's why timing is so important.

Teams usually practice their blocking every chance they get. Good blockers can sometimes score more than half their team's points. When a skill can do that, you had better practice it.

The biggest problem young blockers have is jumping too soon. When that happens, they are already starting down as the spiker reaches the top of his jump and hits the ball. Then the spike often flies over the blocker's fingertips. The block attempt has failed.

Blockers usually stand from one to three feet from the net as they await the play. They should hold their hands at shoulder

Blocking is an important part of to-day's power volleyball game. The most common block is the double block, shown here. But there is also a single block and an occasional triple block. A blocker usually stands from one to three feet from the net in the ready position, hands up. He then approaches the net and takes off from a fairly deep crouch with both feet. When the hands go up, the fingers should be spread slightly and the thumbs almost touching.

height with their elbows tucked in. Then they watch the setter. The blocker must know where the spike will come from, and the setter is the first tip-off.

When the spiker is getting ready to jump, the blocker or blockers must move quickly into position. They must always let the spiker jump first. Then the blockers go up. They use their arms to propel them into the air, then raise both arms straight up, the hands reaching as high as they can go. Fingers are spread and held just a few inches apart.

Blockers are allowed to reach over the net, but not touch it. On an attack block, they will snap their wrists, trying to slam the spike right back to the floor on the other side of the net. With a defensive block, they try to deflect the ball to one of their teammates. Either way, blockers must time their jumps so that they are at the highest point just as the ball is spiked.

With the ideal block, the spike will slam into the heels of the blocker's hands and rebound to the court on the spiker's side of the net. It is helpful if the player cocks his wrists back slightly, so the heels of the hands will point toward the ball.

Blockers are allowed to reach over the net, but not touch it. A blocker who can jump high above the net can use the "reach-over" rule to an advantage. When the blocker reaches over, it's called an *attack block*. The blocker is trying to put the ball back on the spiker's side of the net.

For a blocker who cannot jump as high, the *defensive block* may be a better play. The player should not try to reach over the net. Rather, he should try to control the ball on his side. He wants to get it to a setter so that his team can go for the spike.

There are several ways a team can try to block. One is with a *single block*. That means one blocker going up against the spiker. Then there is the *double block*. Two players go up side by side, putting four hands above the net to stop the spike.

In the double block, one player is usually already in position to go up. But the second player must use some fast footwork to put himself next to the first blocker. Many players use a crossover step to make that quick move for the block. Others will do a sideways shuffle. Use whichever style you feel will get you there faster.

Sometimes both blockers will have to move in opposite directions to reach the point of the spike. This takes teamwork and practice. Both players must stop in the right spot and go up together. One step too many and they can bump into each other. And even the slightest bump will destroy the timing of the jump.

There are even times when all three front-line players go up for the block. This usually occurs when the spike is coming from the midpoint of the net. The three-player block should be used only by experienced teams. For while there is a good chance the block will work, three players in one spot leaves a lot of the court open. A good spiker could beat the block. Then the other players must quickly cover the open spots.

Jumping, timing, teamwork. They are all parts of good blocking. And good blocking is another key to playing volleyball to win.

Learning How To Dive and Roll

As with most other sports, defense plays a big part in a winning volleyball team. No team can win with just offense. There are a number of defensive skills besides the block that every player must know. They are skills that will help save points. There's an old saying that the best offense is a good defense. And that's certainly true to some degree.

In the modern game of volleyball, players often dive and roll around the floor. Sometimes they make great saves that way. Any kind of save made just before the ball hits the floor is called *digging*. A big part of digging is *diving*.

Diving can be an exciting play. But in a sense, the dive is really a fall. The defensive player will start from the ready position. The method is the same for the *dive and roll* as it is for the forearm pass. The player gets low to the court, hands down, and ready to move in any direction.

When the player sees he will have to dive for a ball, he should go off one foot. It is very rare for a player to have to leave the floor before contacting the ball. A player ready to dive will lock his hands and extend his arms the same way he would with the bump pass.

The dive starts with the arms down, pointing to the floor. They should be moved only to swing at the ball. Watching the ball carefully, the player lunges forward by pushing off with one leg. Even with his body almost parallel to the floor, his leg is

54

Left. The dive is one of volleyball's most exciting defensive plays. The player begins as if he is going to make a standard bump pass. Keeping his eyes on the ball, he begins to move forward, hands already in position to make a bump pass. *Right.* As the player steps forward, he keeps his center of gravity low. His arms are kept down, ready to swing up to the ball. His front leg will drive him forward into the ball, while his back leg is held up for balance. Contact is made with the forearms, the same as with the bounce pass.

still pushing. Then he contacts the ball on his forearms by bringing the arms up. This is very important, not only to make the saving hit, but for the follow through as well.

It is the follow through that will break the fall. As the player completes the hit, he extends both arms out in front. Then he brings them down to the court in a position similar to doing a pushup. This will cushion the fall. After touching the floor, he eases himself forward over his arms, arches his back, and lands on his stomach. If this is done right, he will slide forward for a few feet. Then he can jump back up into the ready position.

The dive is a play to save points. With the right technique,

After he swings his arms into the ball, the player follows through by moving his arms forward. His leg drive will also keep his forward momentum going. With this technique, he cannot regain his feet without hitting the floor first.

After the follow through from the hit, the player must quickly extend both arms out in front. This is so he can bring them to the floor in almost the same position as that of a pushup. Because he is still moving forward, this is only to cushion the fall, not stop it. He must lower himself forward over his arms, arch his back, and land on his stomach. It should be a soft landing. If it is done right, he will slide for a few feet on the floor. Then he can jump back up into the ready position.

you won't get hurt. But it takes practice and should be done at first on a mat without the ball. Once you learn the right way to dive and land, then you can begin working with the ball. But stay on the mat until you feel you really have learned the skill. Only then should you try it on the hard floor of the court.

While the dive is used on balls in front of you, the roll is used when you have to move to the side. Once again, you begin in the standard ready position. When you see the ball coming, clasp your hands for the forearm pass.

If the ball is coming to your right, step toward it with the right leg, bending the knee at a ninety degree angle. The left leg is fully extended. You should make contact low to the floor, hitting the ball the same way you would make a bump pass. By this time, the right leg is in a deep squatting position. As soon as the hit is made, pivot toward the target and fall into almost a sitting position.

You will still be moving. So from the sitting position, continue to roll onto your back. Then complete the movement by bringing your legs over the top and making the roll over your left shoulder. If it is done right, you'll come out of the roll on your knees. Then you can jump to your feet quickly and assume the ready position.

The *half roll* is similar to the complete roll except for the final stage. The reach and hit are made exactly the same way. So is the contact with the floor in the sitting position. The difference is that your motion isn't enough to carry you through the full roll. So you must stop and reverse it.

From the sitting position, raise both legs in the air, then tuck them under your knees. Once your feet are on the ground, use your right arm to push yourself back up to your feet and into the ready position. With experience, you'll know right away whether to use the full or half roll.

Sometimes a player can make a bump pass save, but only by lunging, then rolling to do it. With both the full and half roll, the player takes a quick final step to the ball. He then begins to drop the knee closest to the ball, getting his hands ready to lock in position for the bump pass.

There will also be times when you have to try to dig for a ball with one hand. Again, experience will teach you what you can and can't do. You can try a variety of roll and half-roll techniques. But it's best to practice these daring defensive maneuvers on a mat first. Learn the necessary body control and movements. Then start working with the ball, but still on the mat. Finally, you will be ready to put your new skills into action on the court.

A Few Tips About The Game

So far, this book has talked mainly about individual skills. These are the tools every young player needs in order to become part of a team. Then a good coach can show the individual players how to work together to play winning volleyball.

Top. When he makes this kind of hit, the player will be off balance. Instead of trying to break his fall, he just continues to go with his momentum, hitting the floor first with his buttocks. Now he must decide whether to use a full roll or a half roll. *Bottom.* With a half roll, the player will rock a little farther onto his back, kicking his legs in the air. As he starts to come forward, he goes into a body tuck position. To do this, he pulls his legs underneath him and his shoulders back off the floor. When his feet touch the court, he uses his arm to push himself back to his feet. With the full roll, the player kicks upward with his legs and then tucks and rolls back over his shoulder. He ends up in a kneeling position and can jump back up to his feet.

Teams with beginning players will often use a four-spiker, two-setter system, known as a 4-2 offense. It has two spikers at the net and a setter in the middle. Two of the backcourt players will also be spikers and the other a setter. During rotation, there should always be a setter in the front line.

With this system, the team sometimes has to shift positions right after the serve. This should be done if a setter is on one of the sidelines when the play begins. As soon as the serve is made, the setter must shift to the middle, changing spots with a spiker. This will put the setter in a better position to receive the pass.

Good setting is very important in the 4-2 offense. With poor setting, most of the punch will go out of the attack.

Experienced teams rarely use this system, however. They use the three-spiker, or 6-0 offense. That's because everyone on the team is good enough to be a spiker.

And while there are two players whose main role is setter, in the 6-0 that can change. The players are good enough so that the setters can be hitters and hitters can take a pass and make the set.

In this system, the setter will run from the backcourt to the net as soon as the serve is made. That will put four players in the front court: the setter and three spikers. But the setter must be fast. He has to be ready to return to the backcourt and play defense. That's why all players must be cat-quick on the court.

Also in this system, every player must be ready to receive the serve and pass. The main setter usually doesn't receive because he will run into the front line as soon as the ball is hit. So most serves will be handled by one of the two remaining players in the back court. The setter will then have three hitters to work with up front. The 6-0 system can be an exciting attack and is often used when top teams get together.

Defensively, the most popular system is the 2-4. This system has two blockers on the front line and the other four players in the backcourt to dig the ball. Each of the four diggers will cover a section of the court. A good team will vary this system in little ways throughout the game.

Players must always work together defensively. They should use voice signals and try to follow a game plan. A poorly pre-pared team will usually break down on defense first. It really

A good, hard volleyball match may leave players exhausted from all the jumping and diving. But when you win, all that is forgotten. Winning means all the individual skills were working and you played as a team. And that's a great feeling.

takes a great deal of practice to get the defense working smoothly together.

All teams must be very alert on defense. That means knowing where your teammates are at all times, and also where the ball is going. You must always know which area of the court to cover, and which area each of your teammates must cover. If you see one that isn't covered, call it out quickly.

Competitive volleyball is a very fast and complex game. Those who want to play this version of the sport should be ready to work very hard. They must be in excellent physical condition at all times. To tire late in a game means to lose the edge that is very important in volleyball.

But if you don't feel the power game is for you, then you can still enjoy recreational volleyball. In fact, that's the game William Morgan invented nearly 100 years ago. He wanted volleyball to be healthful and fun, and it is for millions of people everywhere.

Yet the game has also become a highly skilled sport, played in many countries of the world. The best players are gifted athletes who take a back seat to no one. If being one of the best is your goal, starting working now. Learn all the skills described here and then practice very hard. Be a team player and listen to your coach. If you do all these things, you'll have a chance to make it to the top.

Glossary

Approach Fast, striding move toward the net by a spiker before he jumps in the air.

Attack Name given to the jumping phase of the spike as the player soars above the net to make the hard hit.

Attack Block A type of block in which the blocking player or players reach over the net to prevent the spike from coming onto their side.

Backcourt The 20-foot area from the end line to the spiking line on each side of the court.

Back Set Type of set made when the spiker is behind the setter. The setter must send the ball directly over his own head.

Backward Pass Pass made when the player's back is to the net and he must send the ball directly over his own head.

Block A defensive play by one, two or three players who leap in the air to try to stop the ball before it passes over the net.

Bump Pass Basic pass in which the ball contacts the tops of the forearms, which are held together by interlocking hands and straight elbows.

Defensive Block Type of block in which the blockers do not reach over the net. The ball is often played to one of the blocker's teammates.

Digging Defensive play in which a player hits the ball just before it strikes the floor.

Dink An attack play in which a player hits a very soft shot over the net when the defense is expecting a spike.

Dive A defensive maneuver in which a player lunges forward to make the hit, then breaks his fall with his hands and lands on his stomach.

Double Hit A foul called when the ball strikes the body twice very rapidly. It can be called on a pass if the hands aren't locked or the forearms are not absolutely flat and level.

Elbow Snap A type of pass in which the elbows are not locked until a split second before the passer makes contact with the ball.

Forearm Pass General name given to a pass in which the ball is hit by the flat surface of the forearms, which are held close together.

Foul   Any violation of the rules resulting in loss of the serve (if call is on the serving team), or scoring of a point (if called against the defensive team).

Held Ball   Violation called when the ball rests on a player's hands or arms for too long a time.

Overhand Floater   Name given to the basic overhand serve in which the ball floats, rather than spins, across the net. It acts much like a knuckleball in baseball.

Overhand Spin   A type of overhand serve in which the server puts spin on the ball to get it to drop or curve.

Pass   Term usually used for the first of three hits by the offensive team. The pass goes to the setter, who then tries to set up the spiker.

Power Volleyball   The competitive style of volleyball started by the Japanese in the 1960s, featuring spiking, diving, jumping and rolling.

Ready Position   The stance in which a player awaits the ball. The player is low to the court, knees bent, feet spread and hands low. He is ready to move quickly in any direction.

Recovery   Term used to describe the movement of a player following a hard spike. He must come down squarely on both feet and be ready to react quickly if the spike is blocked back to him.

Roll   Defensive maneuver also started by the Japanese. It involves moving quickly, then reaching far to the left or right to contact the ball. Recovery is made by falling into almost a sitting position and rolling completely over and jumping back quickly to the ready position.

Server   The player who is serving. Since the players rotate on the court, there is a different server each time the team gets the ball.

Serving Area   The area behind the end line from which the player must serve. It extends 10 feet from the right corner of the court. The player can serve from any point behind this line. But he cannot move to the right or the left of it.

Set   Name given to the second hit of the basic offensive sequence. The set is a soft hit above the net that allows the spiker to jump and hit the ball hard into the defensive court.

Setter   Name given to a player whose job is to set up the spiker by lofting the ball softly above the net.

Side Out   Term used for the loss of service by the offensive team.

Spike   An attacking play in which the ball is slammed hard into the defensive court from above the level of the net.

Spiking Line   A line on the court 10 feet from the center line on each side. Players in the backcourt cannot come up and spike from the area between the spiking line and the net.

ney went to bed.
ossible, she fished
h and toothpaste.
id. "Never," She
Ow!" she yelled.
where Ricky was
clapped over her
d.
y. She spat some-
reat chuckie-stone

"It's green," she

the tube of tooth-
toothpaste," she
bag and produced
d in the middle
s did, and which
toothpaste. Well,"
ere did this come

and began squeez-
y and then large

omething? This is
her old sponge-
out her toothpaste
ou put it back?"
g," said Ricky. "I
g." She hung over

the basin gazing

they be ... *emer*

are these?"

Fay said in a

They were e

thusiasm, Miss F

port, and Londo

Yard, and an ex

hotel and took

before it was all

pillows, exhauste

her face, she had

since she had g

toothpaste in I

Page's. "What a

"What a holida

you?"

"Never," said

Fay as usual

turned over. "To

INFORMATION EXPLORER

SUPER SMART INFORMATION STRATEGIES

HOW TO HANDLE CYBERBULLIES

by Ann Truesdell

CHERRY LAKE PUBLISHING • ANN ARBOR, MICHIGAN

A NOTE TO PARENTS AND TEACHERS: Please remind your children how to stay safe online before they do the activities in this book.

A NOTE TO KIDS: Always remember your safety comes first!

Published in the United States of America
by Cherry Lake Publishing
Ann Arbor, Michigan
www.cherrylakepublishing.com

Content Adviser: Gail Dickinson, PhD, Associate Professor, Old Dominion University, Norfolk, Virginia

Photo Credits: Cover, ©Kamira/Shutterstock, Inc.; page 4, ©karelnoppe/Shutterstock, Inc.; pages 7 and 27, ©JJ pixs/Shutterstock, Inc.; page 9, ©wavebreakmedia/Shutterstock, Inc.; pages 10 and 24, ©ZouZou/Shutterstock, Inc.; page 11, ©Yuri Arcurs/Shutterstoc, Inc.; page 12, ©John Roman Images/Shutterstock, Inc.; page 17, ©Denizo71/Shutterstock, Inc.; page 18, ©Goodluz/Shutterstock, Inc.; page 19, ©Pressmaster/Shutterstock, Inc.; page 28, ©prudkov/Shutterstock, Inc.

Library of Congress Cataloging-in-Publication Data
Truesdell, Ann.
  How to handle cyberbullies / by Ann Truesdell.
      pages cm. — (Information explorer)
  Includes bibliographical references and index.
  Audience: Grade 4 to 6.
  ISBN 978-1-62431-127-7 (lib. bdg.) — ISBN 978-1-62431-193-2 (e-book) —
ISBN 978-1-62431-259-5 (pbk.)
  1. Cyberbullying—Juvenile literature. 2. Internet and children—Juvenile literature.
I. Title.

  HV6773.15.C92T79 2014   2013012344
  302.34'302854678—dc23

Cherry Lake Publishing would like to acknowledge the work of The Partnership for 21st Century Skills. Please visit www.p21.org for more information.

Printed in the United States of America
Corporate Graphics Inc.
July 2013
CLFA13

Table of Contents

CHAPTER ONE
What Is a Cyberbully?

Many kids use tablets and other portable devices to stay in touch with friends over the Internet.

Technology and the Internet have changed the way people live. It is easy to stay in constant contact with our friends and family using e-mail, text messages, and **social networking** sites such as Facebook and Twitter. Most kids and teenagers love being able to keep in touch with their school friends after they've gone home. But technology also makes it so that some kids can never escape the worst part of school—bullying. When kids bully other kids using technology, it is called cyberbullying.

4

When you think about bullying, you might picture one kid physically hurting another kid. But bullying does not always involve physical violence. Bullies can hurt people by insulting, threatening, or teasing them. They can spread rumors, leave people out of activities on purpose, or try to embarrass others. These nonphysical forms of bullying can happen face-to-face. They can also happen when communicating online or with a cell phone. Cyberbullies can hurt people using instant messaging or e-mails. They can post hurtful things about another person on Web sites or blogs for others to read. Some cyberbullies even make fake accounts about the person they are bullying on social networking sites. Then they post lies or embarrassing information about that person. Hurtful rumors can spread very quickly on the Internet.

Mean text messages are just one example of cyberbullying.

You are so ugly. You should not even come to school.

Cyberbullying is always between kids who are under age 18.

Cyberbullying usually happens between kids who go to school together rather than between strangers. But cyberbullies are not always the same kids who bully people offline. Being online can encourage people to do things they wouldn't do in person. People may act differently if they feel **anonymous**. Sometimes they say things online that they would be too afraid or embarrassed to say to another person's face.

People under the age of 18 are called minors. Cyberbullying always involves two minors. If an adult is involved in threatening or hurting kids online, it is not called cyberbullying. It is called harassment or stalking. Get help from a trusted adult immediately if this describes a situation you are in.

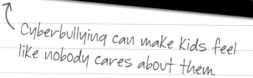

Cyberbullying can make kids feel like nobody cares about them.

Kids who are cyberbullied often feel threatened and alone. Being cyberbullied hurts just as much as being bullied in person, if not more. Targets of cyberbullying may feel like they can never escape the bullying. Even when they go home, insulting text messages or hurtful e-mails follow. The hurtful words are there for them to read again and again.

Bullying of any sort is wrong. So why do some kids cyberbully? What can be done to stop it? What if it happens to you? Read on to find out what you can do to stop cyberbullying.

TRY THIS!

Cyberbullying and offline bullying have a lot in common. Match up the cyberbullying incidents with their offline equivalents.

1. Sending an insulting e-mail to someone
2. Posting a video of a student on YouTube and sharing the link with others so they can make fun of it
3. Posting untrue information about another student on a blog
4. Creating a fake Twitter profile of someone and using it to tweet damaging comments

A. Passing around an embarrassing photo of another kid
B. Spreading rumors about another student at school
C. Mimicking another person in front of others to get a laugh
D. Calling someone names or putting them down

Answers: 1-D, 2-A, 3-B, 4-C

Consider each of the pairs of bullying examples. Do you think cyberbullying hurts more or less than offline bullying? Do you think it's easier for someone to be a cyberbully than an offline bully? Why or why not?

CHAPTER TWO

Why Do Kids Bully?

↑ Sometimes kids begin bullying if they are having problems at home.

Most kids understand that bullying is wrong. So why does it happen? There are some kids who bully others into being their friends, so that they remain the most popular kid in the group. Then there are kids who are not good at making friends or fitting in. Instead, they pick on other kids in an effort to have interactions with others. Kids bully because they are insecure, angry at others, or frustrated by something happening in their personal lives. Some kids are simply bored and choose bullying as a cruel form of entertainment. It is important

Some cyberbullies try to impress their friends by making fun of other kids online.

to try to understand why someone bullies if we want the cyberbullying to stop. There are different methods that work to stop different kinds of cyberbullies.

Many kids cyberbully to make themselves feel powerful. These types of cyberbullies feel like they are better than their targets, and they want their friends to know it. Some kids even cyberbully in groups. They might gather around a computer and pick on another kid using the Internet, sometimes just for entertainment. Cyberbullies who want to brag to their friends about the bullying and who bully in groups are looking for a reaction from their targets. If a target ignores the bullying, it will typically cause the bullying to stop. The cyberbully simply loses interest in that target.

However, it is possible that the bully might move on to another target if the first target does not report the bully. To truly put an end to the bullying, the target should report the incident to a trusted adult.

Cyberbullies are sometimes kids who are trying to get back at another kid. They might be a target of either online or offline bullying themselves. They may be trying to help or protect a friend. These types of cyberbullies may feel like they are doing the right thing. But bullying is wrong no matter what reason the bully has for being mean. These cyberbullies need to get help from an adult to solve the original problem.

It is better to seek help from an adult than to fight back and risk becoming a cyberbully yourself.

Kids who are targets of these cyberbullies might be afraid to get help because they fear that they will get in trouble for what they did wrong in the first place. This might be true, but the bullying situation can get them in even bigger trouble. It is best to talk to a trusted adult about the situation. A school counselor might be able to help the kids involved talk through their issues and find a way to be friends.

Finally, there are cyberbullies who bully by accident. These kids simply do not think things through when using technology. Some kids are pretending to be someone different online. These kids are trying out a new attitude without considering how their words

Think carefully about how your words will make people feel before sending messages or making posts online.

and actions online will affect others. Other kids might go online when they are angry or frustrated and type something unkind that they wouldn't want to say in person. Other times, someone might accidentally send a message to a whole group of people when it was meant for only one person to see.

There are also kids who might hurt others' feelings by accident. When things are written down rather than spoken, they can be read in a way that is different than the writer intended. Something that a person might say jokingly with a smile in real life may seem mean and insulting when written down. Words often need facial expressions to show that they are gentle or playful teasing. For this reason, many people add **emoticons** like :) to their online messages.

Are you as excited about tomorrow's test as I am? ;-)

Emoticons let people know you are only kidding.

TRY THIS!

Don't be a cyberbully yourself. Keep others' feelings in mind when you are bored or angry. Solve problems that you have with others using calm, kind words, or get an adult to help you sort through your feelings together.

Don't cyberbully by accident either. Read your messages carefully before you press Send. Make sure that you are saying what you mean to say. Double-check your wording to be sure that your message will not be misread. Let's practice this skill. How could you change the e-mail below so that you don't accidentally hurt your friend's feelings?

Hey Dave,

I can't believe you got a D on the science test! That stinks. How stupid do you feel? Maybe you should study harder for the next exam. I studied a ton, and I got a B.

Your friend, Paul

Continued on the next page

Your friend might read that e-mail and think that you are making fun of him for getting a bad grade on the test. He might also think that you are actually calling him stupid and then bragging about your own grade. Try to reword it so that your words are polite and helpful instead.

Hey Dave,

I'm sorry to hear that you got a D on the science test. I hope you're not taking this too hard. It was a hard test for me, too. Maybe next time we can study together. Two heads are better than one, right?

Your friend, Paul

To get a copy of this activity, visit www.cherrylakepublishing.com/activities.

CHAPTER THREE
If It Happens to You

You may be angry if you have been cyberbullied.

You are not alone if you are a target of cyberbullying. It is estimated that one in six kids in the United States has been cyberbullied at some point. Even though cyberbullying is common, it is not right. Do not suffer in silence if you are targeted. Take steps to stop the bullying and help yourself heal from the pain.

You may be tempted to respond when you receive a mean message. Your best bet is to not respond to the attack, though. Why? First, bullies crave a response from their targets. It's part of the "game" they are playing. If you do not respond, the bully is likely to get bored with you. He or she might stop. Second, you are likely to be angry or upset when you respond. You might say something in your response that makes you a cyberbully, too.

Even though you should not reply to a cyberbully's messages, you should not delete them. Save them as evidence of the bullying in case it continues. That way you can show proof of what has happened.

No matter how a cyberbully makes you feel, it is always best to not respond.

Keeping quiet about cyberbullying will only make you feel worse.

If you are being cyberbullied, try blocking e-mails or messages from the bully. This will prevent him or her from communicating with you online.

The next step is for you to be open and honest about the bullying with a trusted adult, such as a parent or teacher. Many targets of bullying feel embarrassed or ashamed about the situation. They keep the bullying a secret. Some kids are afraid that they will lose technology privileges at home or school. However, staying quiet can make feelings of sadness and loneliness even worse. If you find yourself in this situation, you should talk about it with a trusted adult. He or she can help you solve your cyberbullying problems.

Show the adult the evidence you have gathered. He or she can help you develop a plan to stop the bullying. Your parents or teachers might assist you with contacting school authorities. Even if the bullying does not happen at school, your principals and counselors can still help. They might not be able to punish the bully, but they can monitor the situation and keep you safe at school. An adult can help you report the cyberbully to the instant messaging program or social networking site where the bullying is occurring. In some cases, the bully's account will be deleted so that the bullying cannot continue in that form. Any physical threats the bully makes should be reported to the police.

Show evidence of cyberbullying to a trusted adult.

If you are cyberbullied, try talking about the problem with your friends.

Even after cyberbullying stops, the targets can still feel hurt. They might feel sad, lonely, and depressed. They might feel unpopular or like they do not fit in with the other kids at school. Many also feel anxious and nervous. This can cause them to become physically sick with headaches and stomachaches. Kids who are bullied often have trouble concentrating at school. Others feel angry and might even resort to bullying others in turn. Continue communicating with your parents or teachers about the situation and about your feelings. Your school counselor can help you deal with your feelings, too. Work hard at making true friends, and be a good friend yourself.

To get a copy of this activity, visit www.cherrylakepublishing.com/activities.

TRY THIS!

If you are a target of cyberbullying, it is important to talk to others about your situation and your feelings. Most kids have been picked on by others at some point in their lives. By talking to others about how we feel when we are hurt, we can deal with pain that we have experienced. You can help others by listening to them.

Talk to a classmate, parent, or teacher about bullying. You can share your experiences and ask them to share their own experiences. Have you ever witnessed someone being bullied? Have you ever been bullied yourself? How did you feel? What did you learn from that experience? How does it change the way that you treat others?

Tell someone!

Some kids worry about how their parents will respond if they tell them they are being bullied. Try to imagine yourself in their position. What if your best friend or a sibling was being bullied? How would you respond to that situation? How would it make you feel?

Don't be afraid to talk!

21

CHAPTER FOUR
Stop It Before It Starts

Don't be a target for cyberbullies!

You can prevent yourself from becoming a target of cyberbullying by practicing the basics of online safety. Always think before you post anything online. Deleting an e-mail or closing a chat window doesn't mean that your words are gone forever. Anything posted on the Internet can be recovered. This includes e-mails and messages that you send to others as well as pictures, videos, and comments that you post. Before you post or send, decide if your message is something that you could share with others without being embarrassed. If you wouldn't share it with many other people, don't post it or send it online. Look at everything you post as something that could potentially embarrass you in the future. Is it truly worth posting that silly picture or rude joke?

Keep your passwords private.

Do not share too much personal information online, even with your friends. Keep your passwords private. Passwords should be shared only with your parents. Your parents can help guide you on the Internet. They want what is best for you. Help them help you by keeping them in the loop. Tell them what you are doing online and listen to their suggestions. They can help keep you safe.

Being safe online might not stop other kids from picking on you. However, it will make it more difficult for them to find you or locate information to use against you. To prevent yourself from being bullied, you should also consider the different reasons that kids bully others. Remember that while some bullies choose their targets for no particular reason, many others bully to get revenge. Make sure that you are a kind person both online and offline. If you have a problem with another student, try to solve it peacefully, perhaps with the help of an adult.

At the same time, you can avoid becoming an accidental cyberbully by practicing simple **netiquette**. Reread everything you write before you hit the Send or Post button to make sure that your message is polite and means what you want it to say. Avoid using bad language, even when joking with friends. Never use another person's username or password. Do not post pictures or videos of others without their permission. Do not pretend to be someone who you are not.

Rereading your text messages before sending them can help you avoid becoming an accidental cyberbully.

To get a copy of this activity, vi
www.cherrylakepublishing.com/act

TRY THIS!

How much information about yourself can you find online? Type your name into a search engine and see what comes up. Try different combinations of your name, such as your full name, nickname plus last name, or first name plus your school name or city and state. Use quotation marks around your name so that the search engine looks for that exact phrase. For example, your search terms might look like this: "Elizabeth Thompson" + "George Washington Middle School."

You might be surprised how much information about yourself there is online.

25

Continued on the next page

Do you see your home address, phone number, or e-mail address online? Can you find pictures or videos of yourself? Can you find a link to your profile or posts on a social networking site? Show an adult what you've uncovered. You can work together to take steps to remove any excess personal information from the Internet.

You might need to change your e-mail address if it is listed on many Web sites. It's also a good idea to leave your last name out of social networking profiles. For example, instead of going by "Elizabeth Marie Thompson," you might make your name just "Elizabeth Marie." If anyone besides your parents or teachers knows your passwords, change them and do not share the new ones with others.

CHAPTER FIVE

Don't Just Stand There!

Don't keep quiet if you see hurtful messages about other people online.

If you are aware of a cyberbullying situation but not actually involved, you are a **bystander**. Bystanders often do not want anyone to get hurt. They still remain silent about cyberbullying, however. Many bystanders don't tell anyone about the bullying they notice because they don't want to be bullied themselves. They might feel like it won't make a difference even if they do step up to help. Being a bystander to bullying can make you feel depressed, worried, and unsafe at school. It also sends a message to the bully that what he or she is doing is OK. It sends a message to the target that no one cares about him or her. Allowing bullies to cause trouble might also make people think that you are a bully, too!

Don't be a bystander. Take a stand against cyberbullying. Tell a trusted adult if you witness or even just suspect cyberbullying. You can also help the situation by letting the target know that he or she is not alone. Be kind to the target and try to include him or her in activities that you do. When bystanders keep quiet, the cyberbullying situation becomes even worse. Speak up and you will show that you care, and that you stand for what is right.

Be friendly to victims of cyberbullying to let them know you care about them.

TRY THIS!

How can we put a stop to cyberbullying for good? Many people believe that bullying is most likely to stop in an environment that does not help it grow. Create a culture of kindness at your school. Begin with yourself. Be accepting of others and their differences. Develop relationships with other students and with the trusted adults in your life.

Let others know that cyberbullying is wrong. Try talking to your teachers or principal about developing programs that help students report cyberbullies and deal with issues that cause cyberbullying to happen. You might even create public service announcement posters or videos to spread the word.

How are you going to take a stand against cyberbullying?

Help spread the word about cyberbullying.

STOP CYBERBULLIES

To get a copy of this activity, visit www.cherrylakepublishing.com/activities.

Glossary

anonymous (uh-NAHN-uh-muhss) made or done by someone not known or named

bystander (BYE-stan-dur) a person who is at a place where something happens to someone else but who is not involved

emoticons (i-MOH-ti-kahnz) small images of faces expressing different emotions, used in e-mail or instant messaging to communicate a feeling or attitude

netiquette (NET-i-kit) rules or guidelines for good online behavior

social networking (SOH-shuhl NET-wur-king) using online services such as Facebook or Twitter to communicate and form relationships with other people

Find Out More

BOOKS

Ludwig, Trudy. *Confessions of a Former Bully*. Berkeley, CA:
   Tricycle Press, 2010.

Polacco, Patricia. *Bully*. New York: G. P. Putnam's Sons, 2012.

WEB SITES

StopBullying.gov

www.stopbullying.gov

This U.S. government Web site offers helpful tips for preventing
bullying and how to respond when you are bullied.

STOP Cyberbullying

www.stopcyberbullying.org

Learn more about why cyberbullying is such a big problem and
what you can do to help stop it.

Index

About the Author

Ann Truesdell is a school library media specialist and teacher in Michigan. She and her husband, Mike, are the proud parents of James, Charlotte, and Matilda. Truesdell enjoys traveling and reading.